Ph. D.s

Ph.D.s

Male and Female
Created He Them

By

LEONARD BACON

Publishers

HARPER & BROTHERS

NEW YORK AND LONDON

MCMXXV

Ph. D. s

Copyright, 1925
By Harper & Brothers
Printed in the U. S. A.

First Edition

A-Z

CONTENTS

PREFACE

SOPHIA TRENTON is reprinted from the proceedings of the chapter of Φ B K established at Leland Stanford Junior University, where the poem was delivered in 1920. The author gratefully acknowledges the chapter's courtesy in permitting him to reprint it.

THE DUNBAR TRAGEDY, however, makes in this volume its first and not improbably its last appearance.

SOPHIA TRENTON
A Moral Poem

"The relation of organism to organism is the most important of all relations."
DARWIN, *The Origin of Species*.

SOPHIA TRENTON

A Moral Poem

"The relation of organism to organism is the most important
of all relations."—DARWIN, *The Origin of Species*.

THE Autumn sun streamed through the lecture-
    room.
  Girls swished into their seats with clicks and clatters.
Without, the trolleys rushed by with a boom,
  As if intent upon tremendous matters.
A gay wind bent the maple's ragged plume
  Against the window, tossing the leaves in tatters.
Sophia Trenton in the foremost row
Felt strange and homesick and extremely low.

She was not like a flower (my heroines
  Are painted as a homely muse dictates),
Nor wicked as the seven deadly sins,
  Nor the sweetest of girl undergraduates.
Nor was she one with ruthless hand that spins
  The twisted thread of other people's fates.
Frankly in talents, as in form and face,
Sophia was a little commonplace.

Still she had freshness and a morning look.
  "Everyone," say the French, "is fair at twenty."
Her bosom, as she bent above her book,
  Had the right curve to please the cognoscenti,
And her mouth's corner had a pleasant crook,
  Implying dimples, when she smiled, in plenty.
She was not smiling now. Of all things human,
Nothing's so lonely as a shy freshwoman.

She thought of the white house in Schuyler Falls
  And morning-glories by the picket fence.
It only made Columbia's clanging halls
  Seem more impersonal and more immense.
Dull times there are when memory appalls.
  And she was overwhelmed by the cold sense
That she had lost more than could e'er be garnered
At Morningside, particularly at Barnard.

She thought of the "apartment," twelve by ten,
  That gave upon the grimy court and chill,
Of a dawn she had not hated until then,
  Of a heavy sun that somehow lacked the will
To scale uninteresting skies again,
  Of coal-dust-flecked milk-bottles on her sill,
Of cats, at midnight in adjacent yards,
Howling their passions much like modern bards.

[4]

Just then all point device, and brisk, and right
    Upon the dot, the lecturer came in—
A startling man to her, for any might
    Have startled her, who checked pale thought within.
Perhaps the future held some haggard light.
    Quiet came o'er the rustle and the din.
It might be glory had not all departed.
A street car clanged far off. The lecture started.

The lecturer's voice was good. Its pleasant sound
    Came sweet upon her ears—a mellow timbre
That suited well his theme somehow, who round
    The mountains of Romance appeared to clamber,
And to walk safe upon enchanted ground
    Where he found treasures of pure gold and amber,
Which he revealed to awestruck contemplation
As the true basis of an education.

The lecture was a poem in its way,
    At least free verse, unusually free,
Although in this it differed, I must say,
    Being allusive in a high degree.
He quoted much from poets grave and gay,
    And his voice leaped when he said "poetry,"
So that Sophia taxed her wandering wit,
Wondering if he perhaps were fond of it.

And much she heard that struck her with amazement,
  Queer phrases full of sounds and fever-heats,
Catchwords of ecstasy and of abasement
  In which the imprisoned spirit throbs and beats.
He slammed the sash of many a magic casement.
  (Little Sophia had not read her Keats,
Although sad Ruth was never more forlorn,
Sick—sick for home amid the alien corn.)

He told them Shelley was the pioneer
  Of spiritual poetry, whose ways
Led over heights so awful that men fear
  To follow—that his verse was all ablaze
With light—and that the pure in spirit hear
  A faëry melody in Adonais,
And the world-revolution's dreadful sound
Trumpeting when Prometheus is unbound.

Then with a swift transition on he went.
  Nothing is swifter than a swift transition;
Not Congress on appropriation bent,
  Nor troops that storm an enemy's position.
Nor financiers on dividends intent,
  Nor the rightabout of a skilled politician.
When changing ground, a lecturer of tact
Beats these and radio—everything in fact.

"The Greeks," he said, "Parthenon—violet crown—
    Sappho"—he lingered with a languorous air
On the words as though he loved them. Up and down
    Her spine she tingled, flushing to her hair.
And though she might have wondered, I must own,
    As Pope says, "how the devil he got there,"
She was much thrilled, instead, though, by the way,
She thought that "Sappho" was a lewd French Play.

Now many a half-thought was half suggested,
    And now he paused on demi-dreams to dwell.
Sophia thought that she was interested,
    Although in what it had been hard to tell.
Somehow she felt the powers of evil bested,
    And the big devil bound fast again in hell
With chains of words, although I can't conjecture
How this could be accomplished by a lecture.

Those Greeks he spoke of—with her shining eyes
    She saw them suddenly. They ceased to be
The half-tone figures of school histories.
    Now they gleamed out upon her flamingly,
Large, gracefully audacious, calm and wise,
    Creatures she thought of, and could almost see
Halfway between the actual and ideal.
Suddenly she knew that they had once been real.

This be it known the lecturer did not know,
   And never had been led even to suspect.
He was not a bad fellow as men go,
   But frankly he was after an effect,
A practice which is apt to bring men low.
   Witness how many poets have been wrecked
Upon that rock. He had woven all his web
Out of the bowels of Sir Richard Jebb

And Gilbert Murray. Twenty years before
   Himself to learning had John Percy given,
A sacrifice to literary lore,
   By the fierce whips of the twin-devils driven,
Poverty and Vanity, who overbore
   Judgment. And it had seemed a glimpse of heaven,
That vision of long academic calm,
Laborious, earnest, pleasant as a palm.

So he was actor on that meaner stage
   Whose sole prop is the professorial chair.
He played his part, expounding many a page
   Where never difficulty lurked in lair.
Thence many a notion did he disengage,
   Especially notions that were not there.
(In the interests of the stricter metricality
Notion I wrote instead of triviality.)

And he was very greatly to be pitied,
   And yet more pitiable, alas! he knew it,
For he had been irrevocably committed
   To talk about a thing and not to do it.
Men suffer thus however nimble-witted,
   And find not, though they seek peace and ensue it,
Their minds in a perpetual bereavement,
Wanting the strong embraces of achievement.

Not that he was not highly publicatious,
   Each year a volume more or less he tallied—
The simulacrum of a book, but, gracious!
   What reader e'er so hardy ever rallied
His forces to the sticking-point audacious,
   And faced that ghost of learning thin and pallid?
Ah! never, never shall that reader be
Saving perhaps another Ph.D.,

Who with great show of learning shall refute
   That which already has been self-refuted,
And multiply the matter in dispute,
   Merely to be himself in turn disputed.
So rushes on the circular pursuit,
   And will, I fear, till Gabriel's horn is tooted.
But the interruption of the Day of Doom
Once o'er, I'm sure the champions will resume.

Here to be frank, like Sterne I own I hanker
    After digressions. This is a confession.
They help one when the cerebellum's blanker
    Than minds of students at the summer session.
When the brains are out, then there is no sheet anchor
    To windward better than a long digression.
And I have noted all men more or less
Display a disposition to digress.

My pseudo-hero, whom I have compounded
    Out of the traits of several men I know,
My pseudo-heroine, in short, dumbfounded.
    She felt her whole mentality aglow.
Her ship was on a sea unknown, unbounded,
    Where the trade-winds of easy doctrine blow
In the mind's tropic. Nor was there one to say
How very near the listless doldrums lay.

That term she harked to Percy's every lecture,
    And read the poets that he indicated,
As if you could by reading them effect your
    Spirit's salvation, and be elevated
To sit with saints in robes of seamless texture.
    And now and then after the hour she waited.
To ask him how she could improve her themes,
And, inadvertently, revealed small dreams,

Shy little verses which were all her art.
   (Briefness was the sole beauty not refused them.)
And Percy in the goodness of his heart
   Quoted them at the Club where he perused them
Each noon, until the ritual grew a part
   Of luncheon. With much humor he abused them.
And poor Sophia's rondelays and ballads
Came on the menu like the fruits and salads.

He said she was a type. Beware of him
   Who says that anybody is a type
Of anything. It means his sight is dim
   And all his fruitage of the mind unripe.
Though Individuals wither—life is grim—
   They yet retain the individual stripe.
And the different manners in which people act
Is what makes up the fun of life in fact.

He sent her to the College Magazine
   With a smart letter to the smart Jew Editor,
Buttering her verse with oleomargarine.
   But she had wanted flattery, and he fed it her,
Till she was happy as a movie queen.
   Never was debtor gratefuller to creditor
For ten days' grace than she, who now by dint
Of her simplicity appeared in print.

[11]

And thus she met the undergraduate poet,
   And worse the undergraduate poetess,
Self-styled originals who thought to show it
   In eccentricity of hair and dress.
"Their aim was moderate, but they hit below it."
   They loved their lucubrations none the less.
And in a downtown tavern once a week
They gathered for high discourse on technique.

Technique! The very word is like the shriek
   Of outraged Art. It is the idiot name
Given to effort by those who are too weak,
   Too weary, or too dull to play the game.
The mighty have no theory of technique,
   But leave it to the blind, the halt, the lame,
"Mental noncombatants," and paralytics,
Second-story men of letters and small critics.

Though why distinguish? Since the birth of time
   Critics have been by definition small,
Wishing rather to commit a little crime
   Than never to commit a crime at all.
Therefore they rob the schoolgirl of her dime,
   But freely give the two-gun man the wall,
Though when he's past, under their breath they mutter
Small insults that aloud they dare not utter.

The Sappho of those Lesbians was a Jewess,
  Swarthy and bosomed like a pouter-pigeon.
Israel is lean sometimes, but what more true is
  Than that maids tend to fat in that religion?
Moses, a lawgiver who surely knew his
  People—in a most unproductive region—
Observed that some waxed fat and were grown thick
And that the corpulent were apt to kick.

And Rachel Stein forsook the God who made her,
  Esteeming lightly the Rock of her Salvation
Just like Jeshurun. From the social nadir
  Of Twentieth Street she had reached the elevation
Of Barnard. She prosed much. Once some one paid her
  For a sloppy article on immigration
And the melting-pot. Accordingly her standing
Throughout Columbia's Grub Street was commanding.

And she was dull, but then her friends were duller.
  She could be silent with a certain patness
Better than speech. And her talk had a color
  That in some sort disguised its natural flatness.
Her Rabbi father thought her beautifuller
  Than Leah, or than Ruth, despite her fatness,
But he was an old man, gentle and kind,
And from reading in the Talmud nearly blind.

Rachel and he had come where the roads fork.
  She was a modern. His was the old law.
It's hard with naught but teeth to pull a cork,
  It's hard for youth to view old worth with awe,
It's hard to be religious in New York.
  His happiness had only known one flaw—
She made a point of being extra chipper
All through the celebration of Yom Kippur.

Sophia found her an enchanting thing,
  Full of suggestions pseudo-oriental.
It was delight to her 'neath Rachel's wing
  To chase ideas small and sentimental,
And sing her song and fling her little fling.
  And Rachel was so comfortable and gentle
That I am much inclined to wonder whether
A softer pair of softs e'er came together.

They were inseparable. They shared in all
  There was to share of pleasure and of lore.
They went to concerts in Carnegie Hall.
  Theirs was one passion for Jack Barrymore.
They heard Caruso bay and Garden squall.
  And Noyes and Masefield thrilled them to the core,
When, night-gown clad, they yielded to the spell
Of many a verse and many a caramel.

And so Sophia grew a Sophomore,
   Emerging moth-like from the gray cocoon
Of pale freshwomanhood. And in a score
   Of ways she showed it. The soft airs of June
   Brought her on rapidly. The Minotaur
   Of Education does not strike too soon.
When the victim's lost in labyrinthine ways,
Leaping from ambush, if he can, he slays.

Now she must choose her specialty. Of course
   She stuck to Percy and the School Romantic,
Drawn to the man by some vague moral force,
   And the hope that if her effort proved gigantic,
He might perhaps her dearest wish indorse,
   Which swelled like the circulation of the *Atlantic,*
And, grant her—O wagon hitched to what a star—
Admission to his Shelley seminar,

When in due season she should graduate.
   Professor Percy kept an eye upon her.
Her found her admiration adequate,
   A sentiment, he felt, which did her honor.
So when revolving years brought round the date,
   And the President's scrawled turkey-tracks were on her
Parchment, and a moderate modiste had fitted her
Sprigged graduation muslin, he admitted her.

And all that summer for twelve golden weeks
   Little Sophia Trenton walked on air,
Having been admitted to that class of freaks,
   Nicknamed by Percy's chief, who had a flair
For pun and epigram, "Percy's Reliques,"
   So many cast schoolmistresses came there,
So many brainless intellectuals drifting
Midway between makeshifting and uplifting.

September came once more. And with September
   Sophia to her oracle returned,
Sunburnt, and full of ardor to dismember
   Shelley till all his mystery she discerned.
In the seminar she blew the little ember
   Of dumb enthusiasm till it burned.
But there was too much mental CO_2,
So even Sophia's flame was rather blue.

At the yellow table-end, delivering doom,
   Sate Percy, chin on hand, calm 'mid their vaporing.
His brow, deep scars of intellectual gloom
   Had temporarily entrenched. Such capering
As made him famous in the lecture room
   He scorned, having now the air of one wall-papering
With perfect taste the chambers of the soul.
They worshiped him in this severer rôle.

The papers that they wrote, they read, alas!
  There was much talk of source and bibliography.
Sophia overwhelmed the wondering class
  With a bright specimen of the new monography,
The subject chosen by herself. It was
  Entitled "Shelley's Knowledge of Geography."
Percy, in whom Shelley ne'er stirred one pulse,
Praised the design, but doubted the results.

Here let me state in categoric terms
  That though he swayed her with a power hypnotic
As a snake's when toward the warbler's nest he squirms,
  Her mind contained no trace of the erotic.
The blow-fly does not mate with angleworms.
  Moreover, Percy had a wife despotic
And moral, who, I am reasonably sure,
Would never have permitted an amour.

But mentally she grew his odalisk,
  A slave in his belles-letterish hareem.
His bland reproof she no more dared to risk,
  Than to have practiced with the football team.
An asteroid, at due distance from the disk
  Of its great primary, would sooner dream
Of breaking from its orbit some fine day,
And doing business in the Milky Way

Than would Sophia of venturing an opinion
  Professor Percy had not guaranteed
As sterling currency in the dominion
  Of Literature. His verdict was her creed.
Scared darkies, fleeing from the Carolinian
  Or Texan Ku Klux, never paid more heed
To their own terror than Sophia paid
To Percy's literary gasconade.

This he saw quickly, and he told his wife
  Of the dimensions of his influence
Upon his students, how he waked to life
  And stirred the sleepy channels of their sense,
Till they were fit for intellectual strife.
  He did not tell her, though, that accidents
Even in that bloodless struggle find a place,
And the ghost of shame and the shadow of disgrace.

His consort snorted as she combed her hair.
  She had heard all that before and was inclined
To say so, but, deciding to forbear,
  Got into bed, apparently resigned
To listen to his tale of how and where
  A thesis-subject came into his mind,
On which to date no specialist had hit,
And how Sophia had just jumped at it.

Sophia had, in fact, as leaps the trout
   Besprent with rainbow dyes, leaped from the stream
Pedantic at the fly, with never a doubt,
   Though it was a brown hackle of a theme
That in her innocence she singled out.
   A change came o'er the spirit of her dream.
There was a shining goal in sight, and she
Resolved to labor for a Ph.D.

Her thesis was—I have forgot—no matter!
   Something she had decided to demonstrate.
Wreaths about Shelley's urn she yearned to scatter,
   Though the victim, had he known, might well remon-
      strate,
For, though in some ways madder than a hatter,
   In normal times he had his headpiece on straight,
And both his eyes had in fine frenzy rolled,
If ever in his life he had been told

That dryasdusts would moralize his song,
   Reading the meaning out and Plato in,
Interpreting the simplest symbol wrong,
   Missing the gold and treasuring the tin,
Dwelling upon the trivial so long,
   And spinning allegory out so thin
That the line parts, and neither brawn nor brain
Can splice the mainbrace of the mind again.

What *was* the theme that Percy had suggested?
  Aha! I have it. The investigations
Of Dowden left one area uninfested,
  Namely, Shelley in his musical relations.
Sophia her small capital invested,
  After some most inspiring conversations
With Percy, in this cramped and arid field,
Which gave no promise of a tenfold yield.

Ah, smile not! There are theses yet absurder
  Than poor Sophia's pile of tinsel tissue.
They move the man of common sense to murder
  Not only the perpetrator, but his issue.
When Folly speaks, be sure the fools have heard her.
  And if you don't believe me, then I wish you
Would read a thesis that displays to us
Wagner's indebtedness to Æschylus.

Sophia's plan was this. She catalogued
  Exhaustively the lines where Shelley made
Mention of music. Shelley's waterlogged
  With music. Through the sun and through the shade
Unweariedly his wingèd words she dogged.
  When he wrote "melody," or "serenade,"
Or "song," or "Music when sweet voices die,"
She tagged them all for reference by and by.

[20]

Heard melodies are sweet, but those unheard
  To her were sweeter. Soon she could detect
Under the mask of almost any word
  Allusion to a musical effect.
She tortured opposites till they concurred
  In sense the poet never could suspect.
And the work sped, and she was never weary
Of her new musical-æsthetic theory.

She drew an interesting parallel
  Between his songs and arias from Gluck
Whose Orpheus drew Eurydice from hell,
  Yet lost her by an inadvertent look.
Haydn and Handel played their part as well.
  Beethoven cut a figure in her book.
She showed—the exposition was a gem—
What Shelley might perhaps have thought of them.

And she was happy, laboring day by day
  With Percy's bland approval for a spur.
Only one obstacle before her lay,
  And it was of a sort that troubled her,
For Rachel Stein, her friend, had gone away
  And much she missed her plump philosopher,
Who was in love with a pale, ineffectual,
And unattractive Christian intellectual,

Who loved the human race, himself in chief.
　　Sophia, sorting literary rubble,
Often gave way to sympathetic grief,
　　As she thought about poor Rachel and her trouble.
She would have died to give her some relief,
　　To have gained her wish, or prick the silly bubble
Of Rachel's tragic, amorous eccentricity,
But could do nothing, which was her felicity.

Another trouble soon upon her grew.
　　The thunder of those battles oversea
With which America had naught to do,
　　Ruffled her meditation fancy free.
She dreamed of them, although she held the view
　　That both sides were as guilty as could be.
This theory, by the way, she had acquired
From Rachel and the man Rachel admired,

Who, though he was the weakest of weak sisters,
　　Yet was in this consistent, for he bragged
That he would be most passive of resisters,
　　If into war America were dragged.
And his tongue soon had calluses and blisters
　　From being so perpetually wagged
And twisted into the convenient attitudes,
Appropriate to pacifistic platitudes.

Our intellectual's name was Dana Phipps,
    And naturally his mind so called, was cluttered
With phrases that came glibly from the lips.
    But poor Sophia felt that he had uttered
Much that was true. Though at this point he slips
    From the tale, she often pondered, as she puttered
At her notes, on his acuteness, and the craft
With which he finally outran the draft.

The folded buds of Nineteen-seventeen
    Brought spices to the April day again,
But few beheld that avenues were green,
    And the bright Spring come in. Men saw too plain
What lay before, and all that it must mean,
    The slaughter, and the pestilence, and pain,
And the hawk famine on destruction's fist.
They saw it all—and hastened to enlist.

The river filled with ships that passed by night,
    Unseen and silent as a thief may come,
Slinking down the darkling flood without a light.
    The college woke to trumpet and to drum,
And dressed itself in khaki trig and tight.
    And overhead Sophia heard the hum
Of aëroplanes that dropped on the bystander
A thousand flying leaves of propaganda.

Sophia's heart was somehow not inclined
    To labor on amid that martial bustle.
She felt as though she had been left behind
    And never would catch up without a hustle.
But Percy reassured her wavering mind.
    With fresh conviction she began to tussle
With piles of references as before,
While Young America went off to War.

Then one June evening as she journeyed lone
    Over a quite unusually arid
Desert of notes, where not the whitened bone
    Remained of any poor idea miscarried,
Her landlady called out, "Miss Trenton—'phone!"
    A voice said: "I am going to be married.
It's Rachel, dear. To-night! We had no warning.
Come right away. He sails to-morrow morning."

Half an hour later mild Sophia found
    Herself in Rachel's new and shining flat.
Upon the hatrack as she gazed around
    She saw a spick-and-span new service-hat.
Rachel—an unknown Rachel—trimly gowned,
    And radiant, and very much less fat,
Swept in. There was a new light in her eyes.
She had been looking at realities.

And close behind her in the garb of war
  A really quite magnificent young Jew,
A sergeant in the quartermaster corps.
  Oh, Dana Phipps! The heart that ached for you,
I'm reasonably sure will ache no more.
  Rachel with an ecstatic gurgle threw
Her arms about Sophia. The embrace
Made up in vigor what it lacked in grace.

Weddings in Nineteen-seventeen were swift.
  Rachel and Moe Rabinovitch were wed
Swiftly as any. The apartment lift
  Bore them downstairs. The waiting taxi fled
To some hotel. A momentary rift
  Let light fall on them through the clouds of dread,
Grimly upon their marriage night withdrawn.
Eight hours were theirs. His leave was up at dawn.

The hollow subway roared and clamored round
  Sophia. Rachel's grief and exaltation
Shocked her almost, as pensive, homeward bound,
  She gave a loose to her imagination.
Life seemed a riddle rather too profound
  To be good taste. She almost passed her station,
She was so lost in thought. I can't say why
Sophia felt greatly inclined to cry.

But her hands shook as she unloosed her hair,
    Alone before the mirror in her room.
And the dumb shadows shifting here and there
    Filled her with vague presentiments of gloom.
The present seemed as empty as despair,
    The future as productive as a tomb.
A dry sob shook her maiden diaphragm.
She went to bed and slumbered like a lamb.

Next morning she was at her task once more.
    As a weed floats in with the tide, so did
Her thesis float in with the tide of war.
    To change the figure, her ephemerid
Developed fast. Its larval stage was o'er.
    Soon it must issue from the chrysalid,
And undertake the adventure that awaits
All inarticulate invertebrates.

She passed her doctorate examination.
    Percy presided over two or three
Faint colleagues, who possessed no information
    Apt to embarrass in the least degree.
Though she had thrilled with dreadful expectation,
    She met the test, and I may say that she
Created a distinctly good impression
Of quiet and painstaking self-possession.

And yet her soul misgave her, for the book
   That went at last to the Columbia Press
Had in the galley proof to her a look
   Of dull and real ineffectiveness.
Percy, to whom her troubled heart she took,
   Laughed lightly at her symptoms of distress,
And when he had their origin inquired,
Said with some sympathy that she was tired.

He was, in fact, the cause of her fatigue,
   Though neither's thought wandered in that direction.
He had meshed her in a spiritual intrigue,
   Where plodding pedantry replaced affection
And humor and all things that are in league
   With natural youth. The months of proof correction
Past in processional of pages rolled,
That made Sophia feel chilly and grown old,

And as if she had missed much. At last her book
   Came out full-blown. It did not cause a ruction.
Physically it had a solid look.
   A thing that lived by literary suction,
A critic, namely, kindly undertook
   To puff it. He quoted from the introduction
And quit. Less florid scribes a value set
Upon the work, to wit, "Three dollars net."

A pebble cast into the central sea
   Would drive a larger wave against the beach
Of the utmost continent. But she was free
   From laboring after things beyond her reach.
Now that her task was done, she hoped that she
   Might have an opportunity to teach.
But Sophia, when she put the millstone by,
Found she regained her freedom with a sigh.

And like a wild thing tamed, that dares not go
   Far from the cage, she lingered still about
The seat of wisdom she had come to know.
   The whole disastrous world was wild without.
But here all things were gradual and slow,
   And one was left at liberty to doubt
Whether one's views on Shelley were of such
Importance as to matter very much.

All that red Fall Sophia dwelt alone
   And solitary in her cloister pale.
Then one dull evening the cracked telephone
   Rang. It was Rachel's voice. A broken wail
Came o'er the wire. The agonizing tone
   Pierced through Sophia like a red-hot nail.
There was another casualty she knew.
What did it matter, fire, or flood, or "flu"?

In the downtown flat she found wild Rachel weeping,
    As once in Ramah, not to be comforted,
Amid a general wreck of light housekeeping.
    Sophia somehow got her into bed.
And when, collapsed, Rachel at length was sleeping,
    She washed the dishes, picked things up, and read
A telegram, delivered in the mail,
Containing no elaborate detail.

Three dreadful days Sophia nursed the wraith
    Of Rachel, and found her ministry exciting,
For washing dishes in the house of death
    Beats any quantity of thesis-writing.
She drew more ardently a fiercer breath,
    Like one among the captains and the fighting.
On the fourth day she sped up town in haste,
To get a nightgown and a clean shirtwaist.

And as she went across town to her train,
    With Rachel in her thought, and Rachel's woe,
The passing crowd went suddenly insane.
    A soldier yelled, "I tell you it is so."
Sirens began to scream like souls in pain.
    From office windows, like a storm of snow,
On the Autumn air came drifts of paper falling
O'er paranoiacs bellowing and bawling

That the war was over. Soldier-boys rocked high
　　On the shoulders of a crowd of yelling "gobs."
Street girls, with meretricious hair awry
　　And tear-tracked rouge, laughed shrill between their
　　　　sobs,
And waved wild arms to the November sky.
　　And hordes and hosts and multitudes and mobs
Stormed up Fifth Avenue with career and caper
Under the cataracts of fluttering paper,

That like the nightmare of a Ph.D.
　　From the thronged windows without stint descended,
Swamping the asphalt in a shallow sea.
　　The city raved hysterical and splendid.
Somehow there was appalling irony
　　With all that desperate rejoicing blended,
For it takes many a Moe Rabinovitch
To tune a people up to concert pitch—

False tidings, too! Two long months dragged away.
　　Rachel at last began somewhat to mend.
Sophia, who had nursed her night and day,
　　Had not an ounce of energy to spend,
And would be ill if she prolonged her stay.
　　She kissed the forehead of her stricken friend,
And after words like ointment sweet departed,
Herself most comfortless and heavy-hearted.

She reached her room. A scanty pile of mail
    Seemed to be all that was expectant of her,
An oil-promoter's legendary tale,
    Four bills, and a review in a brown cover.
Wearily she unknotted her grey veil,
    And with a half mechanic hand turned over
The dreary, drab, manila-wrapped collection,
Which promised no nepenthe for dejection.

There was not much of anything to do.
    She felt she was too tired to go to bed.
A restless lassitude upon her grew,
    And there was a strained feeling in her head.
With trembling hands she picked up the review,
    And without thought or understanding read,
Till with a shock of consciousness she came,
Crusoe-like, on a footprint—her own name.

A flying-man, whose inadvertent "stall"
    Becomes a tail-spin, knows a ghastly thrill
In the first nick of the appalling fall,
    And the just expectation of a spill.
I do not say Sophia had at all
    The same emotion. But her heart stood still
As death, and her sad eyes filled with the tears
Of all the backed-up toil of seven years.

For the reviewer violently ripped
    The veil of her inconsequence away.
There were live scorpions on the lash that whipped
    Her naked spirit in the light of day.
Swift came the arrowy phrases poison-tipped
    With savage indignation, mixed with play
More savage yet, judgment conjoined with gibe.
He held to the tradition of his tribe.

What hurt most was a sentence at the end,
    Where, after having thoroughly disjointed
Her frame of things, he felt that he must mend
    His manners, and accordingly anointed
Her wounds, somewhat in the manner of a friend.
    She quailed before that pity triple-pointed.
He said: "Miss Trenton's venture was ill-starred.
It is a pity she has worked so hard

At so preposterous a task." Sophia
    Dropped the three-column page. Could such things
    be?
Was this indeed the end of her desire?
    Here was another stroke of irony.
A landbird when his storm-struck pinions tire
    Above the waste of infinite purple sea,
And he sinks fluttering through the hopeless air,
Gives way to no more innocent despair.

The keystone in the arch of her distress
  Was that she knew the gay indictment just.
Good measure pressed down, neither more nor less.
  On what a quicksand had she built her trust!
"A gulf—a void—a sense of senselessness"
  Inclosed her. She had written in the dust
A poor scrawl, which the whirlwind from the waste
Had in a moment utterly effaced.

With an "effort like an athlete's" she choked back
  The sentimental sob of her self-pity.
She pulled her trunk out and began to pack.
  She would depart the miserable city.
She would forget that she had been a hack,
  And that Percy once had seemed both wise and witty.
She would go back to Schuyler Falls among
The morning-glories, where once she had been young.

In April dogwood trees would blossom there
  And the young beech put forth, and daffodils
She knew, that come before the swallows dare,
  And the arbutus patches in the hills
Would take with beauty soft winds everywhere.
  She had ground so long at these mechanic mills
For such a nugatory amount of grist
That now she thought it proper to desist.

There were some books that must be carried back
    To the librarian. Without delay
She snatched them up, and took the well-trod track
    For the nine hundredth and last time. Her way
Wound, 'mid the architectural bric-à-brac
    Collegiate, through a lecture hall that lay
Across her path. She passed an open door
And paused, for with a shock she heard once more

A mellow voice uplifted, pleasant, clear,
    That uttered many a seductive phrase,
Fitted to charm the undergraduate ear,
    And set the imagination all ablaze.
"Shelley," the voice said, "was a pioneer
    Of spiritual poetry, whose ways
Lay through a region we approach with awe."
Sophia looked within the room and saw

Amid the throng a girl who sat enthralled,
    With parted lips and fascinated eyes,
And now and then, breathless with interest, scrawled
    Something that struck her with a fresh surprise.
Pity rose in her as the seconds crawled
    Into the overpast eternities.
Then Percy saw her, and whether from repentance
Or other reason, staggered in his sentence.

Their eyes met. But he saw she understood
   That which throughout his lifetime he had striven
To hide. She knew why all the sallow blood
   Flushed in his cheek. She knew that he had driven
Her ship ashore amid a falling flood,
   And what was even more, she had forgiven.
That hurts. "My word," she thought, "the man's a
    bore."
Smiling she turned away and *shut the door*.

THE DUNBAR TRAGEDY

THE DUNBAR TRAGEDY

WHILOME, as cyclopædias tellen us,
    There was a poet who was named Dunbar,
A bard with force and fire in overplus,
    And will to make a song and wit to mar,
A scion of that race penurious
    Born underneath the sober Boreal star,
He rose above their nobles and their kerns,
Scotland's most splendid singer before Burns.

He was a man of courts, that japed for kings,
    Yet had his passionate moments of regret.
Beauty was in him mixed with other things
    Which it is not improper to forget.
He wrought a lively verse in which upsprings
    A melody and impulse living yet,
For men enjoy, whatever they may say,
Something of Horace, and more of Rabelais.

Satire was in him like his blood and bone,
    And pity who is satire's secret friend.
When shrillest and most savage grew his tone
    A gentler touch was somewhere by to mend
The wounds that Walter Kennedy might moan.
    And there our knowledge comes unto an end.
For what was in his fate is not revealed,
Or whether or no he died at Flodden Field.

Four centuries went over with a rush.
    There were Harry the Eighth and great Elizabeth,
And a Reformation, which at the first blush
    Looked like great stuff, though but the dusty death
Of outworn things, that perished in the crush
    Of cheap new notions which were mainly breath,
Rather than true engenderings of the brain,
But none the less caused lots of needless pain.

There was Kepler and Spinosa. There was Bayle,
    Shakespeare and Milton, Corneille and Racine,
There were Wallensteins and Cromwells on a scale
    Surprising, and Gustav Adolph and Christine,
Louis Quatorze that made the nations pale,
    And Newton who made mathematics mean—
Or was it Leibnitz, as the learn'd allow?
I do not give a dx, anyhow.

And several nations rose, and many fell,
　For there were Frederick Second and Voltaire,
Who started Germany the road to hell,
　And France to a maniac region God knows where.
The wars, the policies, were long to tell,
　And dull beyond what any man can bear,
Though the philosophies were worst I'll grant.
As the old jest goes: Clear your mind of Kant.

There came, too, Robespierres and Bonapartes
　With a gigantic train of many a bard,
Goethes and Byrons. When the battle starts
　Voices sing o'er the tumult evil-starred,
Distracted nightingales with broken hearts,
　Descanting in the darkness fierce and hard,
That, cloud-like, on humanity descends.
Where are the poets when the battle ends?

Goethe at Weimar slept, and Heine died,
　Though Wordsworth lived for an infernal time.
A German *hausfrau* down at Windsor kept
　A sort of state ridiculous-sublime.
Statesmen were more than usually inept
　In perpetrating diplomatic crime.
The 'eighties felt a chilling of the blood
As they beheld the 'nineties in the bud.

And in Vienna to his seminar
   Held forth the Herr Professor Schäferlein,
Who was investigating one Dunbar,
   And was very great in eighteen eighty-nine.
Philology had seen him from afar
   And felt the ichor freeze in her divine
Heart—a pale ichor that had lost its color
Ever since the ministrations of Max Muller.

I drop the umlaut for the sake of rhyme,
   And you could not pronounce it, anyhow.
But step with me into that space of time
   Which, as Shaw says, the 'eighties once called "now,"
And think how Schäferlein was in his prime,
   And his neck clothed with thunder, and his brow
Ready for those extraordinary laurels
Which are the prize of literary quarrels.

He was a curious, hasty, little wight,
   Prying, and with that sort of penetration
That, mole-like, burrows in abysmal night,
   Shunning by preference illumination.
A negative something is its inner light,
   The reverse precisely of imagination,
Also a notion that the art of letters
Consists in taking falls out of one's betters.

He could count syllables with any man.
    His tables of weak endings turned you gray.
His "English Metric," if you chance to scan,
    Will make you glad that verse has had its day,
And poetry like all things lives its span
    To perish of congenital decay.
For it was Schäferlein's appointed lot
To be a catalyser of dry rot—

His appointed lot—and yet enthusiasm
    Was in him, and a queer, contagious flame
Burning from some dark subterraneous chasm
    Of personality. For name and fame
Come not to the individual who has 'em
    Just by achievement. And the mighty name
Of Schäferlein owed more to nervous ganglia
Than to any of his articles in *Anglia.*

The very twitching of his brow and hand
    Said to the student: "At least I am sincere
In a pursuit I may not understand,
    Painstaking though my ends may not be clear.
It is not my intention to expand
    Your field of thought. That's not why I am here.
I'm here to pilot cock-boats through a gulf
Of infinite detail in, say—Beowulf.

Oh, wherefore art thou Beowulf? I wonder.
  Nameless barbaric bard, what have you wrought?
Pithecanthropic semi-epic blunder,
  Here and there sullied by a human thought,
Or fancy fainting 'mid dull blood and thunder,
  Feeble, but to the reader overfraught
Like beauty almost, as he plods rebellious,
Cursing the flame that spared Cotton Vitellius.

Who ever read the Beowulf for fun?
  Who ever could, who ever did, who will?
That mote is in our eyes and hides the sun
  Of poetry from children, on whom still
We force the same dull tasks ourselves have done.
  If the first King who heard it did not kill
The scald, I'll bet he checked the eighth-told tale,
Shouting aloud, "For Thor's sake, pass the ale!"

To Schäferlein, of course, this point of view
  Might seem extreme. I own it does to me.
The fatal savage's imperfect clew
  To the labyrinth of life and destiny
Should not be mocked. But the New Stone Age crew
  Who rant about his truth and dignity
To generations of ungenerous youth,
Know little of dignity and less of truth.

Where was I at? Oh yes! Reader, awake!
   At this point I must drag my hero in.
It's an ungraceful task to undertake,
   But positively my story must begin,
Which I am writing largely for his sake.
   (You thank your stars, there is no heroine.)
Allow me to present with some misgiving
John MacIntyre, who is no longer living.

But in those years at the feet of Schäferlein,
   Or, to be accurate, at his right hand,
MacIntyre sat, noting down in a fine
   Italian hand his own conclusions and
The pearls the master cast before the swine
   Who thronged the seminar from every land,
Dull fellows mainly in whom MacIntyre
Found little to interest—nothing to admire.

There were Yankees, there were Frenchmen and Ruthe-
     nians,
   An Oxford Hindu, and a Spanish Jew,
With a sprinkling of Circassians and Armenians,
   And a pair of Irishmen who soon withdrew.
Beowulf aroused their jealousy as Fenians,
   For with a sick foreknowledge they foreknew
That Beowulf, though some may praise unduly,
Is better than "The Cattle-Raid of Cooley."

Two years before John MacIntyre had won
    Cambridge's baccalaureate degree,
And a gold medal splendid as the sun
    For a bright little burst of poetry.
And by the waters of Cambridge many a don
    Made him the theme of radiant prophecy.
And undergraduates garbled all his witticisms,
And a highbrow weekly published his book criticisms.

And furthermore, a London publisher,
    One of that clan so easily beguiled,
Brought out some children of his muse which were
    Limpid, melodious, and undefiled,
Though a sharp lady (it was mean of her)
    Held that he warbled native Oscar Wilde,
An epigram which kept its bitter tang,
In spite of nice reviews by Andrew Lang

And Austin Dobson, and a charming note
    From Mr. Swinburne. Now I don't know why
That woman's word stuck somehow in John's throat,
    Rather like a lump, when one's inclined to cry.
And hard upon it, some cheap critic wrote
    A bit of billingsgate that you or I
Would have forgotten, and with great banality
Bolstered a charge of unoriginality.

[46]

All writers have their masters. All men's thought
    Draws from the one source of the commonplace.
But can you make it poignant as you ought,
    Give it a gentler curve, more delicate grace,
Lend it a meaning clear and subtly wrought,
    Or bring the flush of beauty to its face?
It's something that you probably can't do,
But if you could, were Shakespeare more than you,

Except in mere degree of airy power?
    Of course not! Though of course I must admit
That Wilde's a poet, famous in his hour,
    Who as a master seems to me a bit
Absurd. The green carnation's not a flower
    Which I admire. His melody and wit
Seem to me mere baroque and gilt and plaster.
No, he was never stuff to be a master.

Only a feeble exquisite, idly toying
    With letters or his morbid appetite
By turns, and finding either a bit cloying,
    Amateur poet, amateur Sodomite,
Passionless whether enduring or enjoying,
    Almost magnificent though never quite,
But with enough of artificial fire
To captivate a boy like MacIntyre.

Oh, sucking poets, pause before you pick
  Your masters, and consider, look around.
The polyanthuses are far too thick,
  Darnel and milkweed flourish in all ground.
The poison-ivy festers, cat-briers prick,
  But here and there arbutus may be found.
And sucking poets, if you needs must suck,
Skunk-cabbages are beastly things to pluck.

I speak, of course, wise after the event.
  MacIntyre, blind from many a paragraph
And quatrain brilliant with false ornament,
  No doubt imagined wheat was in the chaff,
And aped perhaps the mien magnificent,
  Leaning unwitting on a rotten staff.
Hence the lady and the critic hurt his pride,
And some Scotch conscientiousness beside.

And like a shot he gave up poetry,
  In spite of the benignant Andrew Lang
And Austin Dobson's soft loquacity,
  And Swinburne's furious, torrent-like harangue.
He tore those pages from his history,
  Nor any song thereafter ever sang.
He was a fool, perhaps, and not the stuff
Of poets, who notoriously are tough.

Instead, he chose to be interpreter
  To others, lecturer, tutor, what you will,
Of all that beauty mere discoverer,
  That in himself it had hurt so to kill.
He would make straight the pathway as it were
  For youth with the authentic lyric thrill
And universal eloquence divine.
So he sought out Professor Schäferlein.

The iron early entered in his soul,
  Already sore from lyrical defeat.
That prosy stuff would chill the Arctic Pole,
  And rob an iceberg of its latent heat.
Twice did the sun around the zodiac roll,
  And yet he sate unsleeping in his seat
At Schäferlein's right hand, and heard afar
The surge and thunder of the seminar.

There raged discourse of arsis and of thesis
  There the Ruthenian battled with the Jew.
There they took Beowulf painfully to pieces,
  And there they reconstructed him anew.
There half-grown morons, stricken with paresis,
  Weekly, laborious papers struggled through,
Which, curious to say, they thought they wrote,
Though they had not enough learning to misquote.

One of the gang had somehow been elected
    To be a sort of scapegoat for the rest,
A pallid twenty-three-year-old dejected,
    Whom semi-weekly Schäferlein oppressed.
Himmelroth was his name, whose misdirected
    Ambition had reduced him to a jest,
A sad and lonely little German burning
With a grievous incapacity for learning.

He haunted MacIntyre like a sad dream.
    His bathos was confoundedly pathetic.
His blunders, which made the intellectuals scream,
    Affected MacIntyre like an emetic.
He helped him struggling with each pedantic theme
    With a Samaritanism energetic,
Though he knew that all his labor was in vain,
It being hopeless to engraft a brain.

For his reward he had admiration dumb
    And inconvenient, and little confidences
Vague dreams concerning happier times to come,
    Vague schemes to meet his small current expenses,
And one day, in a burst of venturesome
    Admission that dispensed with all pretences,
He owned he viewed the far-off doctorate
As preliminary to the marriage state.

MacIntyre used to wonder, as he toiled
    Over the tasks that Schäferlein had set,
About those poor hopes, certain to be foiled
    As anything on which a man could bet.
But scholarship the anaconda coiled
    About him. He would presently forget
Another's troubles, as he ordained the laws
Of Middle English penthemimeral pause,

One of Schäferlein's enigmas, who had said
    Repeatedly to the Frau Schäferlein:
"That Englishman appears to have a head.
    He's quite a help with that Dunbar of mine.
As for the others they are dumb and dead.
    I'll set him to collate the Bannatyne
Recension, and clear up some points perplexed,
That nonplus students of the Maitland text."

Ye Gods, what points! Does "cowffine" mean fine cow
    Especially when set by the word "calf"?
O'er stuff like that MacIntyre bent the brow,
    And did not know whether to weep or laugh,
And in a rotten poem anyhow
    Chaff of the fifteenth-century pornograph,
When he might lightly all his soul engage
With Dunbar shaking in a sacred rage,

Weeping for poets he had loved or known,
  All gone the way of dusty destiny,
From "nobil Chaucer" and Hew of Eglintoun
  To Quintene Schaw and Walter Kennedy,
Estopped in all their beauty one by one
  From ballad-making and from tragedy.
Oh, Timor Mortis, cutting to the quick
The spirit of the bard "quhen he was sick."

Oh, Timor Mortis, greatest of all dreads,
  Except perhaps the fear of being bored,
The empty head's fear of like empty heads,
  The dull mind's natural reaction toward
Similar dullness. When the phantom treads
  Near us, and his opiate-draught at length is poured,
Shall we discover, as the shadows fall,
Death himself is the greatest bore of all?

But MacIntyre could not have held that view,
  While Schäferlein held forth about Dunbar.
He did whatever in him lay to do,
  And interest followed timidly afar,
Although her peacock pinions seldom flew
  Athwart the slumbers of the seminar.
Only at midnight, in his lamp-lit rooms,
MacIntyre heard the rustle of her plumes,

As the poet whom the pedant daily wronged
  Came glimmering in strange splendor to his sight
Out of the past obscure and shadow-thronged
  Of them who knew the art greatly to write,
Till his heart thrilled within him many-songed,
  "A throne of glory in the abyss of light."
Lucky are they who feel inductive fire
Pulse from the great as did John MacIntyre.

And at last there came a vision like ambition,
  A way out, a deliverance, an escape
From erudite and charmless inanition,
  Although it took the questionable shape
Of bringing out a popular edition
  Of the great Dunbar, that should defy the rape
Which the inexorable lecher time
Intends against our empire and our rhyme.

He nursed the project softly in his heart.
  It should be a volume pulsing with afflatus
Of editorial passion, whose chief art
  Is to admire. The learned apparatus
Should dwindle down to a subordinate part.
  The bard should reassume his proper status,
Nor, in a marsh of philologic lore,
Look small by an egregious editor.

I know one thesis duller, Himmelroth's
    Concoction of irrelevance inept,
Entitled "Some Preliminary Notes
    On Barbour." Schäferlein would not accept
That work, and so for once deserves our votes.
    MacIntyre saw the victim as he crept,
Crushed and dejected, from his examination.
His thesis was condemned to publication.

It brought him dubious fame in certain quarters.
    The great George Saintsbury, at the time not great,
Reviewed it furiously, for many waters
    Quench not the embers of prosodic hate.
But there was a fair quota of supporters
    That stood against the foeman in the gate.
Kaluza, Vietor and the dreaded name
Of Cosijn gave him qualified acclaim.

He needed rest after the first sensation
    (Some seven souls had really read the book).
The Schwarzwald suited with his inclination,
    And thither his bewildered way he took,
Chewing the cud of bitter contemplation,
    As a fish mumbles o'er the baited hook.
It's a poor diet, for man cannot feel
Aught sharper than his own soul's barbèd steel.

The beauty all about him made him sicken,
  As he thought upon the thing that he had done.
Three years of work, and not one pulse would quicken
  For all his labor, no cheek flush—not one.
He could half feel tangible darkness thicken
  About him, standing in the morning sun,
A pillar of cloud eclipsing the bright day.
Three years of youth are hell to throw away.

And what thing should a man do to retrieve?
  So did he ponder, watching declining fire
Perish under Venus one cloud-rampired eve.
  After such failure dared one still aspire?
Was there yet left adventure to achieve?
  Could the brain imagine, or the heart desire?
And was it that unnatural Fate but mocked her
Sad child, when she brought mail for the Herr Doctor?

It cheered his Ph. Damnèd loneliness
  And changed the current of his bitter mind
That some one knew his name and his address.
  And he was startled from his revery blind,
For the great Master of Martyrhouse, no less
  Had written to know if he would be inclined
To educate a stiff-necked generation,
Under the auspices of that foundation.

Why Martyrhouse desired him God may know.
  The purpose of the dynasty then reigning
Is purest Attic Greek to me, although
  They said they wanted men with German training,
New blood, and new ideas. It may be so,
  Though the phrase "German training" needs ex-
    plaining.
Foreign devices may confound our taste,
But why let native methods go to waste?

But it was water of life to MacIntyre.
  A burden as it were fell from his brain.
He could not sleep that night, feeling the fire
  Of a new purpose in his soul again.
Flowers yet might bloom in philologic mire.
  Even his book was not all written in vain.
Happily he tossed all night till the larks towered
Melodious out of silence dewy-houred.

He went back to Vienna the next day,
  Where for the last time he saw Schäferlein,
Who quite objected to his going away,
  But with alacrity agreed to dine
With MacIntyre in a small gay café.
  There the great man selected a great wine,
Appropriate to his eminence and dignity,
And drank three-quarters of it with benignity.

They had a curious, not unpleasant time
   In spite of their imperfect sympathies.
It's true they talked of Middle English rhyme,
   A subject which in my opinion is
A good deal more ridiculous than sublime.
   But the good wine diverted them from this,
When MacIntyre, chancing to look around,
Beheld a man, his eyes bent on the ground

Three or four tables off. He somehow felt,
   Though it may have been but influence of wine,
The shadow of things dark that seemed to melt
   Into his sense. A shiver up his spine
Rippled as he beheld strange gloom that dwelt
   Upon a well-known face, grown saturnine
And even more obtuse and pessimistic,
With the eyebrows curved in half-moons Wertheristic.

He looked. It was Himmelroth beyond a doubt,
   Moping alone as was his wont to do.
MacIntyre wondered what he was about
   As the boy fell scribbling over the menu.
Schäferlein, turning, also spied him out
   As Himmelroth with a quick motion drew
Something from his pocket. Ere you could say Jack
Robinson, the room thrilled with the whiplash crack

And shuddering knock that pistols make indoors.
   Women screamed and fainted. Men leaped to their
      feet,
Chairs grided a harsh thunder on the floors.
   Mustached policemen dashed in from the street
In squads and companies and army corps,
   And there was pandemonium complete.
MacIntyre crossed the apartment with a bound
And raised the slumping body from the ground.

Under his eye as he got it into a chair
   He saw scrawled over the red-blotched menu:
"Pardon this mess. Unhappy love affair."
   A surgeon came, and MacIntyre withdrew.
Schäferlein followed him with a wild glare,
   As Himmelroth unhappily came to.
It's come to your attention, like as not,
That the suicide is seldom a good shot.

Even Schäferlein when they were well outside
   Displayed emotion. As they trod the way
Homeward, he argued against suicide,
   Feeling apparently compelled to say
Something. The gust of agony, of pride
   Cast down, of aspiration gone astray,
Struck him as lunacy and nothing more.
MacIntyre, as he left him at his door,

Could hear him muttering, *"Schrecklich,"* as men mutter
   Over matters that they cannot understand,
Taking to speech, when their brains begin to stutter.
   John wondered, "Might not brave men, with fierce
      hand,
Seeing the light of inner being gutter,
   Properly quench the inefficient brand?
Poor Ass!" But 'twas incongruously pat
That such a scene should end three years like that.

Cambridge! What's in a name? I'll tell you what!
   Almost everything that white men care about
Is in that name which makes the cheek grow hot
   To think on. Stately beauty that can flout
Even English centuries hangs round the spot,
   And sacred influence distilling out
The attar of sweet memory o'er the stream
Where Milton, Newton, Byron wont to dream

Dreams quite opposed in character, I'll grant.
   Magic is seated there, though many a don
Lays ghosts effectively, as the shadows slant
   And the remorseless lecture hammers on,
And freshmen vote philosophy is cant
   Silently, in harmonious unison.
For there are men as dull within that pale
As e'er held forth at Harvard or at Yale,

Perhaps even duller, for the British Dullness
  Is facile princeps, just like British Brilliance
And much less rare. There is a depth and fullness
  About it, positive absence of resilience,
And a polished quality of pure numskullness
  In army, navy, clergy, and civilians,
And the flower of imbecility unstained
In the university where it is trained.

And still the beauty and the delicate air
  Enchants those regions, till I half believe
That even the dullest soul transported there
  Gives out such radiance as it may receive,
A fire divine, drifting from otherwhere,
  Any Prometheus might be glad to thieve,
A light almost illuming asininity
Of silver-plated youth at King's and Trinity.

MacIntyre lapsed into that beauty and calm,
  As a tropic fish long wandering might do,
That at last swims again 'twixt isles of palm
  Feeling blue warmth of water heat anew
Dulled faculty. His whole soul sang a psalm,
  And a resurgent beauty thrilled him through.
The lads who read beneath his ægis found
With him a pathway to enchanted ground,

And laughter that too seldom goes with learning
    In these sad times—though where should laughter be
More happily at home than when discerning
    How undiscerning is humanity,
Or how, when highest wisdom's torch is burning,
    Grindstones are hideous things through which to see.
And if we do see through them, then distortion
Of the image seen is laughter's proper portion.

Even his colleagues liked him on the whole.
    He kept his end well up in common room,
When the decanter glimmered like a coal
    And port allayed the academic gloom.
Peace and tobacco comforted his soul,
    And talk full of allusions that illume
Even the darkness of their souls who are
Lost in the various variants of Dunbar.

For the edition was going forward now.
    Martyrhouse's Master favored the design,
Bending on MacIntyre benignant brow,
    Though the history of the drama was his line.
The proofsheets were a slough through which to plow.
    Nor all the honors of the Muses nine
Would move my soul to edit e'er a bard
Upon whose text I had to work so hard.

[63]

I'd rather write an epic any day
  Than put one classic lyric through the press.
I may add that I have done it by the way,
  And stick to the position, none the less.
In spite of what my critics have to say,
  Or haven't, which is worse I must confess.
But then I never did forswear the fire
Divine (perhaps I should) like MacIntyre.

Michaelmas, Lent, and Easter glided by.
  He had labored like a Trojan or a stoker.
A lectureship's no Epicurus' stye
  And even editing contains a joker
Not visible always to the casual eye.
  He had overdone. Indignant nature spoke her
Mind about learning. Sleeplessness, hot and numb,
Taught him life's not all "breve somnium."

The long vacation found him worn and jaded
  From burning learning's candle at both ends.
The Master his fierce industry upbraided,
  And sent him off to Cornwall to a friend's.
But labor still as leisure masqueraded.
  He spent the summer as a spendthrift spends
His fortune, unto the last drop and particle,
In writing what was really a good article

[64]

On the demigod Dunbar. Why no man knows,
   But this, at any rate, is verity
That a man must suffer who turns away to prose
   Even from mediocre poetry.
Some element of surrender I suppose
   Defeats his triumph in its infancy.
Better write hecatombs of lifeless rhymes
Than flinch and be the Dowden of the times.

There is a beauty, but it is still-born
   Over those pages that are buried now,
Some thin forgotten music of a horn
   Echoing far out of Elfland. But somehow
You read the thing with a faint touch of scorn,
   And a regretful wrinkle of the brow,
That the hand to learned dye has been subdued
That might have harped in faëry solitude.

Something of the same thought it may have been,
   When Michaelmas made gay the elms once more,
Brought MacIntyre anew, with saddened mien,
   To plow the Cambridge furrow as before.
His eye was sultry and his cheek was lean.
   And the Master, as his kind eyes wandered o'er
That grievous face, wondered, as Masters will,
Why on earth Dunbar should make a Fellow ill.

For a Master he was greatly exercised,
  Nor the explanation altogether missed.
"A poet manqué," he soliloquised,
  "With a corresponding intellectual twist."
But then at Cambridge one's not authorized
  To be an utter sentimentalist.
The Master meditated what to do
And found no way, no more than I or you.

Though a sharp Dean, whose rôle it was to play
  An airy Pollux to his heavy Castor,
Confided to me once quite by the way
  That he never really understood the Master,
Till the latter in dern privacy one day
  Took counsel with him to avert disaster
Thread-hung above young MacIntyre. Now and then
Intuition touches hearts in heavy men.

Of course they could not estimate the strains
  Shearing the young man's spiritual material,
But none the less the Master racked his brains
  To smooth his path with counsel magisterial,
And had the boy promoted. For his pains
  He got a smile embarrassed and funereal
That scarce knew what to do with so much kindness,
And left the Master cursing his own blindness,

And rather angry to be so distressed
  About the misery of a neurotic,
Who only needed exercise and rest.
  "Those men," he thought, "whose curves are asymp-
      totic
To the normal, can't be helped when they're depressed.
  All I can do is only a narcotic
To him. He's got to suffer and endure.
And, after all, time is a certain cure."

So did he reason while the mountain press
  Labored with the mouse of MacIntyre at last.
The work would issue in a month or less,
  The Master, having read the proof, forecast
In any case a reasonable success,
  Which yet might quench the trouble of the past,
When a book reached him one day in the mail
In all respects much like a cotton bale—

Schäferlein's vasty quarto on Dunbar,
  Note-deserts, with oases of the text
Scattered between them, very few and far,
  The whole with problematic points perplexed.
Over all Dullness like a baleful star
  Brooded. The Master was distinctly vexed
By the contretemps, but as he read ahead,
"Why, MacIntyre is a made man," he said.

"This is hocus-pocus. His is a real book,
   Distinguished, simple, sticking to the fact.
That German's balderdash won't have a hook
   To hang by, all of *schwärmerei* compact.
MacIntyre's is as limpid as a brook.
   This is a swollen, vulgar cataract
Of nothing in particular, bolstered out
To make the heart sick, and a volume stout."

Literary prophecy is a dangerous trade.
   But for once the Master could not be far wrong,
For MacIntyre, in the book that he had made,
   Had kept in mind the singer and the song,
And did not make an imbecile parade
   Of learning. And accordingly a throng
Of literary critics professorial
Paraded theirs after usage immemorial.

Forcing their comment with some importunity
   On the æsthetic-literary press.
But they admitted with surprising unity
   It was a fine performance none the less.
And in fact several took the opportunity
   Their patriotic notions to express,
Proclaiming with discrimination fine
MacIntyre's triumph over Schäferlein,

Which did not please John MacIntyre at all,
  Who had stated clearly in the proper place
His debt to the pedant philological,
  With an appropriate and pleasant grace,
And did not wish a literary brawl.
  Odorous caparisons in any case
Were beastly things which he did not desire,
That being the nature of John MacIntyre.

He sent a copy off to Schäferlein
  And a note in which he said how much he owed
To old instruction in his fresh design,
  And far too much consideration showed
For the feelings of the old man asinine,
  Whom critics said he had passed upon the road.
He dreamed of critics in the deadly night,
Critics who praised one, and were never right.

Now that his book was out, each imperfection
  That he alone perhaps had eyes to see,
Haunted him like a passion. The detection
  Of flaws became habitual, and he
Added daily, to a miserable collection,
  New evidence of imbecility.
He did not know, of course, that he was ill.
People as sick as he was, never will.

At last the Master saw his duty plain,
　And sent him off to Granchester to rest,
A hamlet murmurous with the refrain
　Of a mill-stream playing through the quiet blest,
Unpoeted as yet. His weary brain
　And the sore heart palpitating in his breast
Seemed to slow down together, as he drew
Sweet country breath into his lungs anew.

There is I think no simile that serves
　To express the fact, to them that do not know,
Of the relief terrific of worn nerves,
　When the sick man at the end of strength lets go,
Caring no longer whither the ship swerves,
　Or sink or swim, or lose or overthrow.
But though relief comes, with it, I may add,
Comes too the critical moment good or bad.

But the Master in the common room that night
　A jovial and benignant aspect wore,
And was in his best vein of humor, quite
　As if he had tripped up the Vice-Chancellor
With an epigram divinely in the right.
　He sported like a playful dinosaur,
Chasing its tail in a prehistoric sea.
Dons smiled at his Jurassic repartee.

News of the invalid's progress now and then
   Reached him. Complete collapse had been averted.
Letters he wrote, for melancholy men
   Escape thus from the valley of death deserted.
MacIntyre always had a graceful pen,
   And little fountains of gay fancy spirted
Here and there on the pages, or between
The lines the Master read unto the Dean.

Months passed away as months will pass in colleges.
   December came with her due rain and sleet.
The Master has a weakness he acknowledges.
   He forgot that he expected Doctor Keat
The Chaucerian to dine. Profuse apologies
   He offered to the Doctor, and cold meat.
Keat was quite nice about it, for the wine
Was of a sort to make one glad to dine

With Barmecides. Supper over, by the fire
   They chatted in contentment all benign
That comes when skies are foul and ways are mire,
   Till Keat said: "Have you seen what Schäferlein
Has written in *Anglia* about MacIntyre?
   It's a queer business, and it's none of mine,
Though I confess I should be glad to take
The cudgels up for the young fellow's sake."

The Master snatched up that uncut review,
  Which few of its subscribers ever read.
With a forefinger he rent the pages through,
  And found the hand of Schäferlein indeed.
More obvious venom never yet did spew
  The Gila monster in the loco weed.
The startled Master marveled as he read
At the green jealousy of the gray head.

The crabbèd rhetoric wound to a dull close
  Where it was quite implied, if not quite stated,
In a malignant period operose,
  That his former student had hypothecated
His happier touches from the mass of those
  Laborious researches consecrated
He had had access to, when he pursued
'Neath Schäferlein the paths of rectitude.

"Phew," said the Master laying down the sheet,
  With a beetling brow and an Homeric nod,
"Was there ever more contemptible conceit?
  The Fool hath said in his heart 'There is no God.'
I wish you'd answer him in public, Keat.
  I mean to give the beast a private prod.
To expose himself so! Why, it's unbelievable
And in a scholar, too. Quite inconceivable."

The wind morosely rattled at the pane.
　Keat rose and left, having agreed to write
The answer, and departed through a rain
　That spat like vampires on Walpurgis' night.
The Master, full of sacred and profane
　Fury, took up his pen for to endite.
But on the lifted weapon dried the ink.
He was so angry that he could not think

Save of a nerve-sick man in Granchester.
　He gave the letter up, and went to bed,
But could not sleep. His intellectuals were
　Too much stirred up. Anew the thing he read,
And straight resolved to see the sufferer,
　And tell him what he thought, and what Keat said,
Which should assuredly delight his ear.
He slept at last. Morning came bright and clear,

"With crystal air and sapphire firmament,"
　In the ornamented manner of Dunbar.
The Master rose, and true to his intent
　He drove afield to Granchester afar.
Relieved in mind, he whistled as he went,
　And like a god descended from his car,
While the village ceased its idling customary
To view the splendor of the dignitary.

Not even the restrained and tragic note
　　That the Master, giving up his first design
Like a gentleman, out of death's shadow wrote,
　　Struck home quite to Professor Schäferlein.
He muttered, *"Schrecklich, schrecklich!"* in his throat,
　　His darkness being palpable as thine,
Tremendous Night, descending without star.
Whilome there was a Poet named Dunbar.